Little People, **BIG DREAMS**

GEORGIA O'KEEFFE

Written by
Mª Isabel Sánchez Vegara

Illustrated by
Erica Salcedo

Lincoln
Children's Books

Little Georgia grew up with six brothers and sisters on a farm near Sun Prairie, Wisconsin. But while they played games, Georgia preferred to look at the world around her.

At school, Georgia was always more inspired by the colors she saw through the classroom window than the numbers written on the blackboard.

And when Georgia was 12, she told her mother she wanted to become an artist. She started lessons, and her drawings soon became the most impressive in the class.

Georgia moved to Chicago, and then New York, to keep studying art. But everyone in the city was busy. They didn't have time to notice beauty in the little things around them—little things like...a flower!

So she decided to paint that tiny flower by putting her nose very close to it. Suddenly, the littlest flower became the most enormous painting! No one could ignore its beauty.

A famous photographer named Alfred saw Georgia's paintings and wanted to share her work with the world. He put together an exhibition of her artwork.

Georgia's paintings left the public wide-eyed in amazement. They just couldn't figure out what they were looking at.

But Alfred understood her paintings.
He was an artist, too.

Soon, they realized they were made for each other and got married.

Inspired by New York, Georgia decided to paint towering skyscrapers as only a child would have painted them. For her, the city was made of enormous squares.

And when summer came, Georgia visited New Mexico. She immediately fell in love with the desert. She painted crosses, sand dunes, and even the skulls of dead animals. They were all fascinating to her.

She loved every stone, every bone,
and every color of the lonely desert.
She painted every single day in a house
nestled between red hills. Nothing was too
small or too ordinary for her.

Through her art, Georgia flew all around the world to different museums. They called her the "Mother of American Modernism."

And today, you can see how the ordinary becomes extraordinary, when you take the time to look at it as little Georgia did.

GEORGIA O'KEEFFE

(Born 1887 • Died 1986)

1903

1918

Georgia O'Keeffe grew up on a farm in Sun Prairie, Wisconsin, with six brothers and sisters. From a young age, she was fascinated by the natural world. She decided she wanted to be an artist and began lessons at the age of 12. Her independent spirit took her to Chicago and then New York to study painting. After this, she moved to Texas to teach but kept on working on her own art, creating abstract drawings in charcoal. These drawings expressed her feelings about objects in shapes and lines—rather than looking exactly like the objects themselves. They were very new and different than the drawings of the time in America. She mailed them to a friend, who showed them to the famous

1932

1962

photographer, Alfred Stieglitz. He exhibited Georgia's art at his
gallery in New York, which helped catapult her to success. She later
fell in love with Stieglitz, and they married. Georgia showed her
vision of the world through her paintings. She painted towering
New York skyscrapers, blue-green lakes, and magnified flowers
on giant canvases. Later in life, she made the first of many visits
to New Mexico. This landscape was very influential, and Georgia
spent hours outside painting the red mountains and animal bones
she saw there. She felt truly at home in her ranch between the
desert hills. Georgia's unique style made her one of the most
influential and remarkable painters of the 20th century.

Want to find out more about **Georgia O'Keeffe?**
Read one of these great books:

My Name is Georgia by Jeannette Winter
Meet Georgia by Marina Muun
Georgia's Bones by Jen Bryant and Bethanne Andersen

If you're in Sante Fe, New Mexico, you could even visit the Georgia O'Keeffe Museum to see some of her artwork and the objects and places that she loved.

Brimming with creative inspiration, how-to projects, and useful information to enrich your everyday life, Quarto Knows is a favorite destination for those pursuing their interests and passions. Visit our site and dig deeper with our books into your area of interest: Quarto Creates, Quarto Cooks, Quarto Homes, Quarto Lives, Quarto Drives, Quarto Explores, Quarto Gifts, or Quarto Kids.

Text © 2018 Mª Isabel Sánchez Vegara. Illustrations © 2018 Erica Salcedo.

First Published in the UK in 2018 by Lincoln Children's Books, an imprint of The Quarto Group.

400 First Avenue North, Suite 400, Minneapolis, MN 55401, USA.

T (612) 344-8100 F (612) 344-8692 **www.QuartoKnows.com**

First Published in Spain in 2018 under the title Pequeña & Grande Georgia O'Keeffe

by Alba Editorial, s.l.u., Baixada de Sant Miquel, 1, 08002 Barcelona

www.albaeditorial.es

All rights reserved.

Published by arrangement with Alba Editorial, s.l.u. Translation rights arranged by IMC Agència Literària, SL

All rights reserved.

A catalog record for this book is available from the British Library.

ISBN 978-1-78603-122-8

The illustrations were created with digital techniques. Set in Futura BT.

Published by Rachel Williams • Designed by Karissa Santos
Edited by Katy Flint • Production by Jenny Cundill

Manufactured in Guangdong, China CC072018

9 8 7 6 5 4 3

Photographic acknowledgments (pages 28-29, from left to right): 1. Unknown Photographer. Georgia O'Keeffe, 1903. Gelatin silver print. Georgia O'Keeffe Museum. Gift of the Georgia O'Keeffe Museum Foundation. 2. Alfred Stieglitz. Georgia O'Keeffe, 1918. Platinum/palladium print. Georgia O'Keeffe Museum. Gift of The Georgia O'Keeffe Foundation. 3. Alfred Stieglitz. Georgia O'Keeffe, 1932. Gelatin silver print. Georgia O'Keeffe Museum. Gift of The Georgia O'Keeffe Foundation. 4. Georgia O'Keeffe, 1962 © copyright Granger Historical Picture Archive / Alamy Stock Photo.

Also in the *Little People,* **BIG DREAMS** series:

FRIDA KAHLO

ISBN: 978-1-84780-783-0

Meet Frida Kahlo, one of the best artists of the twentieth century.

COCO CHANEL

ISBN: 978-1-84780-784-7

Discover the life of Coco Chanel, the famous fashion designer.

MAYA ANGELOU

ISBN: 978-1-84780-889-9

Read about Maya Angelou—one of the world's most loved writers.

AMELIA EARHART

ISBN: 978-1-84780-888-2

Learn about Amelia Earhart—the first female to fly solo over the Atlantic.

AGATHA CHRISTIE

ISBN: 978-1-78603-220-1

Meet the queen of the imaginative mystery—Agatha Christie.

MARIE CURIE

ISBN: 978-1-84780-962-9

Be introduced to Marie Curie, the Nobel Prize–winning scientist.

ROSA PARKS

ISBN: 978-1-78603-018-4

Discover the life of Rosa Parks, the first lady of the civil rights movement.

AUDREY HEPBURN

ISBN: 978-1-78603-053-5

Learn about the iconic actress and humanitarian—Audrey Hepburn.

EMMELINE PANKHURST

ISBN: 978-1-78603-020-7

Meet Emmeline Pankhurst, the suffragette who helped women get the vote.

ELLA FITZGERALD

ISBN: 978-1-78603-087-0

Meet Ella Fitzgerald, the pioneering jazz singer and musician.

ADA LOVELACE

ISBN: 978-1-78603-076-4

Read all about Ada Lovelace, the first computer programmer.

JANE AUSTEN

ISBN: 978-1-78603-120-4

Discover the life of Jane Austen, the beloved English writer.

HARRIET TUBMAN

ISBN: 978-1-78603-227-0

Learn about Harriet Tubman, who led hundreds of slaves to freedom.